T0209903

Teaching the Boring Stuff Series

COMMAS

Teaching Students to Use Commas Correctly, Without Boring Them to Tears

Randy Larson

Illustrated by Judy Larson

Routledge
Taylor & Francis Group

NEW YORK AND LONDON

First published in 1999 by Prufrock Press Inc.

Published 2021 by Routledge
605 Third Avenue, New York, NY 10017
2 Park Square, Milton Park, Abingdon, Oxon OX14 4RN

Routledge is an imprint of the Taylor & Francis Group, an informa business

ISBN 13: 978-1-877673-38-2 (pbk)

TABLE OF CONTENTS

How to Use this Book.. 5

Comma Short Course—The Basics in 12 Easy Lessons 7

    Commas after introductory elements... 8

    Commas with interrupting elements... 12

    Commas with ending elements... 14

    Commas in a series.. 16

    Commas in compound sentences.. 18

    Commas in addresses, dates, titles and letters 20

    Commas with coordinate adjectives... 28

Practice Exercises and Quizzes... 31

    Commas after introductory elements... 32

    Commas with interrupting elements... 37

    Commas with ending elements... 44

    Commas in a series.. 48

    Commas in compound sentences.. 52

    Commas in addresses, dates, titles and letters 56

    Commas with coordinate adjectives... 58

Cumulative Reviews and Test 61

Answer Keys... 65

HOW TO USE THIS BOOK

No one wants to spend an entire year teaching commas. Although *Commas* may look, at first glance, like "overkill," it really is not. *Commas* is designed to be a resource book to fit many situations. It is designed to teach the correct use of commas, of course, but also much more—specifically, to teach students about sentence structure. It is designed to give them practice *writing* and *using* language, while at the same time exercising their imaginations and appealing to their sense of humor.

The book is divided into four sections:

COMMA SHORT COURSE. The lessons in the Short Course summarize the basics about comma usage in sensible, easy-to-understand language. For many classrooms, the Short Course is all that is needed to give students a basic working knowledge of comma rules.

PRACTICE EXERCISES AND QUIZZES. Turn to page 31, "Practice Exercises and Quizzes," if you find that students need more work in a certain area. Here you will find supplementary lessons, arranged according to subject area, that will give your students further practice. For example, if you find that students need a better understanding of using commas in a series, they can turn to pages 48–51, which include activities with the header "Commas in a series." Each subject area also includes a quiz.

CUMULATIVE REVIEWS AND TEST. The last section of the book includes cumulative reviews and a cumulative test. These reviews and the test cover all the basics about the correct use of commas.

ANSWER KEYS. Answer keys for all the exercises are included in the last section of the book.

Commas can be used in a variety of ways, depending upon your classroom situation and the needs of your students.

Reproduce the Short Course exercises for the overhead projector, and introduce a lesson every week or so. Most lessons are short and can be done in ten or fifteen minutes. Follow up with practice exercises throughout the year to help students retain what they have learned.

Or, if you prefer to do a complete comma unit at one time, select activities from the book to suit the needs of your students. One idea is to use an activity from the Short Course as a lesson on the overhead at the beginning of class, followed by a photocopied lesson from "Practice Exercises and Quizzes" for students to complete on their own.

Commas sums up the rules about comma usage in a sensible, no-nonsense style that won't bore students to death. Don't be surprised if they learn far more than with traditional exercises from your classroom textbook!

Comma Short Course

Course

The Basics in 12 Easy Lessons

USE A COMMA AFTER INTRODUCTORY ELEMENTS IN A SENTENCE

Surprisingly, Maxine won first place at the Punctuation Festival for her soothing new tune, "Comma Tose."

FIRST THINGS FIRST

Sentences often begin with a little something extra—a word that doesn't quite flow with the rest of the sentence. Sometimes that word is the name of the person you are talking to. Example:

> **Chandler**, *I would like to buy your ferret.*

Sometimes it is a word like *well, oh,* or *however*—something that doesn't quite fit with the rest of the sentence. Example:

> **Well**, *I guess I'd like to try frog legs.*

To show that a word is extra, it is set off with a comma. That means, of course, that the comma goes *after* the word. A few more examples:

> **Marvella**, *would you marry me?*
> **Yes**, *I would love to marry you.*
> **Well**, *maybe I could marry you. Let me think about it.*
> **Sam**, *it is possible that I may marry you. Let me think about it a few months.*
> **Incidentally**, *Tyrone asked me to marry him last week.*
> **No**, *I wouldn't marry you if you were the last man on Earth.*

PUNCTUATE

Add commas as needed to the sentences below. (If a sentence doesn't need a comma, don't add one.)

1. Well I for one do not know any stand-up librarians.
2. Sadly he took his bassoon and went home.
3. No there's nothing wrong with Aunt Louise.

WRITE YOUR OWN

Write two sentences of your own, each beginning with an introductory word that needs to be set off with a comma. Choose from these introductory words: *however, Tammy, yes, Jake, reluctantly, amazingly, besides, happily, no, why, my.*

1. _____

_____

_____

2. _____

_____

_____

SHORT STUFF

Many sentences begin with introductory "stuff" that doesn't quite flow with the rest of the sentence. Sometimes the "stuff" is a short group of words called a phrase or a clause.* An introductory phrase or clause is set off from the rest of the sentence with a comma. Examples:

> *In the back of the refrigerator*, *a moldy jar of mayonnaise sat beside a plate of greenish-looking pork chops.*

> *After sitting through five classes*, *Zachary didn't really want to go with his father to a lecture called "Fun with Calculus."*

PUNCTUATE

Add commas as needed to the sentences below. (If a sentence doesn't need a comma, don't add one.)

1. Oddly enough I've grown fond of milk toast.
2. Practically speaking I wouldn't own a blender if my life depended on it.
3. Although he denies it I'm not at all surprised that Paul ate your Jell-O.

WRITE YOUR OWN

Write two sentences about something that is green, using any of the introductory phrases below.

> *just for kicks • strangely enough • without thinking*
> *in the middle of the day • in the middle of dinner*
> *in the middle of the pond • after eating our dinner*

1. _____

_____

2. _____

_____

* What is the difference between a phrase and a clause? A clause has a subject and a verb. A phrase does not, though it may have either a subject *or* a verb.

LONG STUFF

Introductory phrases and clauses can be short, like *By the way* or *When he laughed*. They can also be very long, sometimes even longer than the main part of the sentence. Example:

> *By the time Angelo ate all the cheese dip and finished most of the chocolate-covered pretzels in the bowl on the coffee table*, the party was over.

All of the words in bold are part of an introductory clause. The comma separates these words from the main part of the sentence, which is *the party was over*.

Another example:

> *If you eat a lot of candy of any kind and never floss or brush your teeth*, your teeth may rot.

PUNCTUATE

Add commas as needed to the sentences below. (If a sentence doesn't need a comma, don't add one.)

1. If you ever have a chance to meet my parakeet skip it.
2. While we watched Allison lunge for the aquarium that was about to topple off the table we all held our breath.
3. In the event of a worldwide lettuce shortage eat cabbage.

WRITE YOUR OWN

Add a long-winded introductory phrase or clause to each of the short sentences below. Start your introductory phrase or clause with one of the words in the box. Be sure to use commas correctly.

---

if • when • while • although • after • because

---

1. _____ I love oatmeal pie.

2. _____ she sleeps past noon.

3. _____ a skateboard would make a great gift.

USE A COMMA TO SEPARATE AN INTERRUPTING ELEMENT FROM THE REST OF THE SENTENCE

Millie Shimbo, the pastry chef for Moose Lodge #121, used a secret ingredient in her Fluff Deluxe cookies.

INTERRUPTERS

Here is a perfectly good sentence:

LaMont and his brother walked to school on Monday.

You already know that you could add an introductory word or group of words to the beginning of such a sentence. Examples:

Yes, *LaMont and his brother walked to school on Monday.*
After they stopped at three convenience stores, *LaMont and his brother walked to school on Monday.*

It is also possible to add a word or group of words somewhere in the middle of the sentence, interrupting the flow of the sentence. Examples:

LaMont and his brother, **incidentally**, *walked to school on Monday.*
LaMont and his brother, **by the way**, *walked to school on Monday.*
LaMont and his brother, **the one who usually drove his car**, *walked to school on Monday.*

Notice that the commas are placed on both sides of the interrupting word or words.

PUNCTUATE

Add commas as needed to the sentences below. (If a sentence doesn't need a comma, don't add one.)

1. No one in the school however knew that Bill's middle name was "Noodles."
2. The Titanic an unsinkable ship sank.
3. My brother thinks that cauliflower the world's friendliest vegetable goes well with chocolate sauce.
4. Mrs. Gymtoe after being hypnotized by Professor Drool during an assembly fell off the stage into a pile of seventh graders.
5. The most important thing the astronauts took to the moon not counting a ton of powdered vegetables was a shiny roll of duct tape.

WRITE YOUR OWN

Write three sentences about a space craft landing on your block. Include an interrupting element in each sentence.

_____

_____

_____

_____

Use a comma to separate an ending element from the rest of the sentence

Miss Tugwell gave all her customers the same haircut, at least most of the time.

ENDING STUFF

You have already learned about introductory words at the beginning of sentences and interrupting elements in the middle of sentences.

"Stuff" can also be tacked on to the end of sentences. A word, a phrase or a clause can come *after* the main part of the sentence. Examples:

> *I want another cookie,* **Mom.**
> *I want it now,* **by the way.**
> *My favorite kind of cookie is oatmeal,* **incidentally.**
> *I love oatmeal cookies,* **the kind with both raisins and nuts.**
> *Mom cooked a huge meal,* **at the same time balancing the check book.**

PUNCTUATE

Add commas as needed to the sentences below. (If a sentence doesn't need a comma, don't add one.)

1. You are my fondest memory by the way.
2. I must have that lobster in the window the one with the sumptuous tail.
3. I never expected you to tell everyone Harvey.
4. You can't go to the movies in that ridiculous outfit Melanie.
5. I like ridiculous outfits Mom.

WRITE YOUR OWN

Write three sentences of your own that include ending "stuff." Build all three sentences around the subject "annoying things that drive me crazy." Choose from the following ending elements:

> *incidentally • on the other hand • Ellie*
> *which makes me grit my teeth • the habit I hate the most*
> *by the way • making me want to scream*

_____

_____

_____

_____

_____

_____

USE COMMAS TO SEPARATE ITEMS IN A SERIES

*Fish, ice cream, burritos and coffee are the specialty
of the house at Eduardo's Exquisite Cuisine.*

LISTS AND LISTS

Imagine seeing *fish ice cream burritos* and *chocolate cake* on the school menu. Fish ice cream sounds bad enough, but fish ice cream *burritos*?

Commas can change the menu entirely. A menu with *fish, ice cream, burritos* and *chocolate cake* sounds a little more appetizing.

The commas, of course, make the difference, serving as little dividers. Whenever you have a list (or a *series*) of items, you need to separate them so that they don't run into one another. You can separate them with the words *and* or *or*, or you can separate them with commas.* Example:

No: *Calvin liked sausage cereal and prune tarts for breakfast.*
Yes: *Calvin liked sausage, cereal and prune tarts for breakfast.*
or
*Calvin liked sausage **and** cereal **and** prune tarts for breakfast.*

PUNCTUATE

Add commas as needed to the sentences below. (If a sentence doesn't need a comma, don't add one.)

1. Max is clever wise wonderfully funny and good with gorillas.
2. Uncle Farley is rich weird whiny and handy with a plunger.
3. Maria used her babysitting money to buy face powder bubble gum fly spray and Oreos.

WRITE YOUR OWN

Now write two sentences of your own that include a series. Make one of the sentences on the subject of *sports* and one on the subject of *desserts*.

1. _____

_____

2. _____

_____

* With the last item in a series, you can use a comma before the *and* if you want. In many publications in the United States, that comma is not used anymore. Either way is correct.

USE A COMMA — ALONG WITH THE CONNECTING WORD AND, BUT, OR, FOR, OR NOR — TO SEPARATE THE TWO PARTS OF A COMPOUND SENTENCE

Ms. Maybird enjoyed her chickens, and she loved feeding them "brain food."

COMPOUNDS

Have you ever had a compound fracture in your arm or leg? A compound fracture means you have not one but *two* breaks in your bone. A compound sentence means that you have not one but *two* parts to your sentence. If you want to get fancy, you can call those "parts" independent clauses.

Here's a simple sentence with one independent clause:

Alexis ate an enchilada.

That sentence is a simple sentence. It is also an independent clause. That means it can stand alone. Now let's look at another independent clause:

Armand gobbled up four tacos and an order of refried beans.

That's another simple sentence. It is also an independent clause.

Now, suppose we put the two sentences above together, with the word "and":

Alexis ate an enchilada, **and** *Armand gobbled up four tacos and an order of refried beans.*

Now we have two complete sentences (or independent clauses), connected with the word *and*.

That brings us to a comma rule. In a compound sentence, put a comma *before* the connecting word *and, but, or, for, nor* or *yet*.

PUNCTUATE

Add commas as needed to the sentences below. (If a sentence doesn't need a comma, don't add one.) Remember, you only need the comma with the connecting word if you are separating two independent clauses.

1. Turkeys are not exactly known for their great brain power and nobody thinks that worms are likely to win scholarships to Harvard.
2. He hated television and music but he loved doing algebra equations more than anything on Earth.
3. Mary and Joe went on a hike up the Absolom Canyon on a beautiful fall day.

WRITE YOUR OWN

Write two compound sentences of your own, using the subject *things that go "splat."*

1. _____

_____

2. _____

_____

USE A COMMA BETWEEN THE DIFFERENT PARTS OF A DATE

*To usher in the dog days of summer, Bernie married Polly
at the Purina Community Center on August 14, 1999.*

DATES

Numbers can be confusing, especially when there are a whole string of them together. That's why we often use commas—to help make the numbers easier to read. For example, 520,000 is much easier to read than 520000.

The same thing holds true for dates. You need a comma between the day and the year, just to make it easier to read. January 2 1999 might be misread, if you were in a hurry, as January 21. Just to keep things straight, the comma is generally used. (Yes, there are some new methods of writing dates that are becoming more common, like *21 January 1999*. For most ordinary writing, however, the traditional commas between the date and the year are used.)

Most people can remember that little comma between the day and the year. What they don't realize, quite often, is that there should be another comma after the year. That comma sets the year off from the rest of the sentence. Examples:

*Cheryl was born on **February 2, 1949,** in a little town in southern Colorado.*

*Damion began taking accordion lessons on **October 23, 1996,** because his grandfather thought he should carry on a family tradition.*

PUNCTUATE

Add commas as needed to the sentences below. (If a sentence doesn't need a comma, don't add one.)

1. On December 4 1289 a Roman teenager invented the world's first dating service.
2. Years ago on November 1 1988 Elvira Twang decided that by January 12 2044 she would have her own hypnotist's shop in downtown Potato Springs.
3. When the mud races began on June 4 1995 Edna was ready with self-cleaning eyeglasses.
4. It was early on the morning of May 5 1888 that Alfred J. Oops learned the meaning of the concept "hazardous waste."
5. At midnight on August 13 1957 Alvin Andrews dreamed of frozen cabbage burgers.

WRITE YOUR OWN

Write two sentences about dates that have some significance in *your* life.

1. _____

_____

2. _____

_____

PLACE A COMMA BETWEEN EACH PART OF AN ADDRESS, EXCEPT FOR THE STATE AND ZIP CODE

The ad read, "Antonio's Blimp Painting School,
401 Last Avenue, Dillpot, Delaware 19898."

ADDRESSES

Commas are useful for separating things. In addresses, the commas help keep all the different parts from running into one another.

For example, suppose you live at 126 Breakwater Drive, Timmonsville, Illinois 53321. The comma keeps the street address from running into the city. Another comma keeps the city from running into the state. Another comma…oops! Why isn't there a comma keeping the state from running into the ZIP code?

Blame it on the U.S. Post Office. Until 1963, addresses didn't have ZIP codes. Then the rule was perfectly clear: Each part of the address was separated from the other parts with a comma. In a perfect world, the post office would have been sensitive to students and how hard it is to learn punctuation rules. It would have said, "Let's separate the ZIP code from the rest of the address with a comma, just as we do the other parts of the address."

Unfortunately, the post office didn't think about students. The people in charge decided on no comma before the ZIP code.

So now, instead of a nice, simple rule like, "Place a comma between each part of an address," you get to learn a more complicated rule: "Place a comma between each part of an address, *except* for the state and the ZIP code."

Note: Some people don't understand what is meant by a "part" of an address. The house number and street are considered one part (126 Breakwater Drive). The city is another part (Timmonsville). The state is another part (Illinois). The ZIP code is another (53321).

PUNCTUATE

Add commas as needed to the sentences below. (If a sentence doesn't need a comma, don't add one.)

1. Send your complaints to Mary Snookum 141 Peewee Drive Hickory Arkansas 72065.
2. Please send my refund to 6543 Hullabaloo Lane Fort Almost Texas 78514.
3. No one can tell the future except the Snapple salesman who lives at 44321 Anxious Avenue Mystic Florida 34221.
4. If your zeppelin lands a little early, stop by and see me at 99887 Elbow Lane Loosejaw Alaska 99604.

WRITE YOUR OWN

Write a sentence of your own that includes the complete address of a person you know. Write another that includes the complete address of a place that you visit frequently.

_____

_____

_____

USE A COMMA AFTER A NAME FOLLOWED BY JR., SR., OR ABBREVIATED TITLES LIKE M.D.

Mattie McGuire, Ph.D., was famous for her abbreviated art technique called "splotch and splatter."

JR., SR. AND TITLES

When a person's name includes an abbreviated title like *M.D.*, *Jr.* or *Sr.*, the abbreviations are separated from the rest of the name with a comma. Example:

> *Melvin Schwinnbaum,* **M.D.**, *and Lawrence Gutting,* **Jr.**, *are in charge of training at the National Kissing Contest in Balderdash, Wisconsin.*

PUNCTUATE

Add commas as needed to the sentences below. (If a sentence doesn't need a comma, don't add one.)

1. Otto Rizzuto Jr. has discovered that the number of people who die from meatloaf overdose equals the number of people who work for Wal-Mart but actually shop at Kmart.
2. For Teacher of the Year I recommend Archie Sprinkler Ed.D. for his contribution to wood shop technology and the invention of decorative flowers made from used hamburger wrappers.
3. Sergeant Emily Strong R.N. is the best nurse in Company D.
4. Before you throw her off the flying insect committee, let it be known that Imelda Johnson Ph.D. was the first to make anti-mosquito powder from dried clam shells.
5. Nobody knows how much work Axel Backfill Ph.D. put into the invention of spray toothpaste.

WRITE YOUR OWN

Marion Fendlehessy just had a baby boy and named him after her husband, Seymour. Write a sentence about baby Seymour, using his complete name. Write another about the doctor, Milton Garcia, using his complete name and title.

1. _____

_____

2. _____

_____

USE A COMMA AFTER THE SALUTATION OF A FRIENDLY LETTER AND AFTER THE CLOSING OF EITHER A FRIENDLY LETTER OR A BUSINESS LETTER.

Dear Mr. Lund,

Please buy a new elephant. This one leaks.

Sincerely,

Ralph Hoopitt

LETTERS

In friendly letters, use a comma after the *Dear* part of the letter (called the salutation). Also use a comma after the closing. Example:

Dear Mary,
   Please write soon. I miss you.
Love,
Garth

In a business letter, use a comma after the closing. However, use a colon instead of a comma after the salutation. Example:

Dear Dr. Jones:
   The bill you sent me is incorrect. You charged me for two visits instead of
   one.
Sincerely,
Leonora Martinez

PUNCTUATE

Add commas as needed to the letters below. (If a letter doesn't need a comma, don't add one.)

Dear darling mice

I'm sorry about your missing tails. My wife went a little crazy when she got her credit card bill for a new set of steak knives, and you just happened to get in the way. I have a brother in Sausalito who is a plastic surgeon. He would be happy to reconstruct your tails. Please contact him at 778-777-8891. He only works on Saturday.

Sincerely
Farmer Hopkins

Dear Cinderella

We miss you terribly. We spent so many joyful hours watching you clean the fireplace ashes and dust under our beds. Please accept our apology for any dirt we may have caused you to get under your fingernails. Mother would like to see your castle, and if you would invite us to the next ball we would bring you some turnip cookies. Kiss the prince for us since we will never get to.

Love

Your two stepsisters and Ma

Dear Cable-O-Rama President

Please cancel my cable television subscription. I am very dissatisfied with your service and can't take it anymore.

Sincerely
Raynelda Murphy

Use a comma to separate coordinate adjectives before a noun

One more comma to go and Ork's long, difficult sentence would be complete.

SIDE BY SIDE

An adjective is a describing word. When two adjectives occur side by side in a sentence, they are called coordinate adjectives and should be separated with a comma. If the word *and* or *or* separates two adjectives, then no comma is needed. Examples:

Comma: *Tall, red-haired stranger*
                Playful, cuddly puppy
                Cold, windy days don't bother me much.

No comma: *Cold and windy days don't bother me much.*
                   Beautiful and intelligent woman
                   Conceited and snobbish chairman

PUNCTUATE

Add commas as needed to the sentences below. (If a sentence doesn't need a comma, don't add one.)

1. Nobody saw the rumpled lonely pigeon sitting on the statue's nose.
2. It was a dark and stormy night.
3. Nobody believed his weary pointless lies.
4. The lonely and dejected slug sat on a soggy bun.
5. Jeff ate an attractive steamy bowl of Spam nuggets.

WRITE YOUR OWN

Write a sentence that uses two adjectives to describe a pizza in a positive way. Write another sentence that uses two adjectives to describe a pizza in a negative way.

1. _____

_____

2. _____

_____

Practice Exercises and Quizzes

ADDRESSING DIRECTLY

Sometimes the introductory element in a sentence is the name of the person someone is talking to. Example:

Susan, bring me a cup of coffee.

Notice that "Susan" is an introductory word. A comma sets it off from the rest of the sentence.

Warning: Don't get mixed up and put a comma after every name you see at the beginning of a sentence. Use a comma with a name only when someone is being directly addressed.

No: *Spike, kicked the football.* (Spike is not being addressed. Spike is not an introductory word.)

Yes: *Spike, will you stop messing around and kick that football?* (Spike is being addressed. Spike is an introductory word.)

PUNCTUATE

Add commas as needed to the sentences below. (If a sentence doesn't need a comma, don't add one.)

1. Mom could I please have more of that delicious broccoli and oyster casserole?
2. Linda wants to exchange her brothers for some new ones.
3. Linda wants a new fur-lined lunch box for her birthday.
4. Linda get over here and wash this turtle!
5. Ira don't you want to dance at the bar mitzvah?

WRITE YOUR OWN

Write two sentences that involve a person named Alex. In one sentence, directly address Alex. Make the other sentence *about* Alex.

1. _____

_____

2. _____

_____

PARENTHETICALLY SPEAKING

The English language includes many words and phrases that are used again and again as side remarks. These expressions are called parenthetical expressions. (If you want to remember the name, think of *parentheses*. Things you put in parentheses are usually extra, just like *parenthetical* expressions.) Some common parenthetical expressions are *by the way, on the other hand, therefore, nevertheless* and *to tell you the truth*.

When it comes at the beginning of a sentence, a parenthetical expression should be followed by a comma. Examples:

> **On the other hand**, *I do not like green eggs and ham.*
> **By the way**, *I forgot to tell you about the tornado.*
> **In my opinion**, *you should turn off the blender. Now!*
> **To tell you the truth**, *I'd be thrilled to get at least one A on my report card.*

PUNCTUATE

Add commas as needed to the sentences below. (If a sentence doesn't need a comma, don't add one.)

1. To tell you the truth I've learned more from my grandpa than anyone.
2. On second thought I've learned a lot from my pet hamster, Richard.
3. In my opinion he's a tough little rodent.
4. In short I'm thrilled with his performance on the XK3000 Whirler Coaster.
5. In fact once he starts spinning, the fur really flies.

WRITE YOUR OWN

Write a sentence about fast food, using any of the following parenthetical expressions as an introduction: *however, by the way, in my opinion, to tell you the truth, on the other hand, therefore, in fact, of course.*

_____

_____

_____

_____

_____

_____

LONG AND SHORT OF IT

Introductory elements need to be separated from the main part of the sentence with a comma. Introductory elements can be short groups of words or long groups of words or even just one word. Here are a few examples:

If you want, I can bring all my little friends.
Within 60 seconds, his head was filled with improper fractions.
Being a thoughtful student, Maxine brought an apple for Ms. Wooldown.
Because school lunches always look so unappetizing and taste so unpleasant, Max always chews Pepto Bismol gum.
Yes, I would love a hot fudge sundae with whipped cream.

PUNCTUATE

Add commas as needed to the sentences below. (If a sentence doesn't need a comma, don't add one.)

1. When you think about it decimals are just periods with a math education.
2. Of all the scientific principles around today I like gravity the best.
3. Beans with red sauce are better than corn dogs on a stick.
4. I can't believe you're the only person in the park with a piccolo.
5. After sneaking into the house later than he should have and being pretty sure his parents hadn't woken up Chuck accidentally kicked the cat.

WRITE YOUR OWN

Write two sentences of your own, using introductory phrases to begin your sentence. Choose from the introductory phrases in the gray box.

> *During what seemed like a six-hour lecture about protons and neutrons*
> *When you eat cake with licorice frosting*
> *Since you seem to like the color beige so much*
> *By the time Angelo ate all the cheese dip and Triscuits*
> *After her little sister got into her make-up bag*
> *Whenever Mr. Markuson saw a yapping poodle*

1. _____

_____

2. _____

_____

A RULE TO REMEMBER

Introductory words are set off from the rest of a sentence with a comma.

- An introductory element can consist of one word. (**Oh**, *I do love geography.*)

- An introductory element can be a person's name, used to show that you are addressing that person. (**Lenore**, *I want you home by 11:00 sharp!*)

- Introductory words can consist of a short two or three word *phrase* or *clause*. (**By the way**, *I didn't pass seventh grade.*)

- Introductory words can consist of a long *phrase* or *clause*. (**After I saw the giant squid's eye peering through the bathroom window**, *I knew I was in trouble.*)

PUNCTUATE

Add commas as needed to the sentences below. (If a sentence doesn't need a comma, don't add one.)

1. Thinking back I would say that Harold was too close to the edge.
2. Tyrone just call her and ask her.
3. Oh I can't wait to bake you some Spam muffins!
4. In the future keep your cuckoo in the closet.
5. By the way you left your little brother at the car wash.
6. If you want I could fix you some creamed turnips.
7. Peter picked a peck of pickled peppers.
8. While under the boardwalk he found Waldo's retainer.

WRITE YOUR OWN

Write four sentences of your own that have introductory words set off with a comma. Build the sentence around the subject of unusual pets.

1. _____

_____

2. _____

_____

3. _____

_____

4. _____

_____

QUIZ

What makes him tick? This is the question haunting all who know or have met Melvin the Magnificent, the alligator wrestler from southern Louisiana. Below are answers Melvin gave to reporters' questions, just before heading off to the National Alligator Wrestling Finals. Add commas as needed to Melvin's answers. (If a sentence doesn't need a comma, don't add one.)

1. After I finish a wrestling match I like to sit down with a Twinkie and a quart of Kool-Aid.
2. When I first got started in wrestling I couldn't get a good grip on their snouts.
3. Before my career took off I used to wait tables in Louie's Lizard Lounge shine shoes at the Algonquin Hotel and play the accordion for tips in the subway station.
4. When I have free time I like to go shopping for alligator ties alligator boots and alligator wallets.
5. If I had it to do all over again I would forget alligator wrestling and become an encyclopedia salesman a used car salesman or maybe an English teacher.
6. Alligators aren't all that smart.
7. Because I have become famous every alligator from here to Africa wants to wrestle me.
8. No I never eat alligator stew.
9. Mary I don't think you should eat alligator stew either.
10. By the way I don't think anyone should eat alligator stew.

WRITE YOUR OWN

Write three questions that the reporters asked Melvin. Remember — this is a crowd of reporters, and they need to get Melvin's attention.

1. _____

   _____

2. _____

   _____

3. _____

   _____

PARENTHETICAL EXPRESSIONS

You have already learned about parenthetical expressions that occur at the beginning of a sentence. Parenthetical expressions are words or phrases like *by the way, on the other hand, therefore, nevertheless* or *to tell the truth*. (If you want to remember the name, think of *parentheses*. Things you put in *parentheses* are usually extra, just like *parenthetical expressions*.) Example:

> *My little sister ate a bite and then threw up.* **However**, *she had warned us that she hated peas.*

Parenthetical expressions can also occur somewhere in the middle of a sentence. They break the "flow" of the sentence and need commas to set them off — on both sides. Example:

> *Arnold,* **by the way**, *is a member of the Royal Sauerkraut Society.*

PUNCTUATE

Add commas as needed to the sentences below. (If a sentence doesn't need a comma, don't add one.)

1. Nobody in our class in my opinion is a match for Burnell Beetlebaum.
2. Nobody except Marlene to tell you the truth can eat 14 sub sandwiches while riding a pogo stick.
3. It seems strange on the other hand that Marlene even owns a pogo stick.
4. I can't of course go with you to the Mushroom Festival.
5. I can't believe even if I wanted to that you're guilty of grand chocolate theft.
6. No one in my opinion should believe her story about the flying fur ball!

WRITE YOUR OWN

Write a sentence of your own that includes a pigeon and an interrupting parenthetical expression. Choose from any of the following parenthetical expressions: *as a matter of fact, after all, for example, however, in the first place, of course, on the other hand, to tell the truth.*

_____

_____

_____

_____

_____

DIRECT ADDRESS

Suppose that Samantha says this:

> Yes, **Jack**, I love you.

The word "Jack" interrupts her sentence and needs to be set off on both sides by commas.

Suppose that Samantha has a nickname for Jack: Snookums. (Yes, it's a bad nickname, but people in love don't always notice such things.) Then she might write this:

> Yes, **Snookums**, I love you.

Or she might use a generic sort of endearment instead of his name, like this:

> Yes, **darling**, I love you.

No matter what Samantha calls Jack, his name needs to be set off on both sides with commas. Whenever you *directly address* someone, using his name or a nickname, you set off that name or nickname with commas. If you are just talking *about* someone, you don't set off her name with commas.

> Commas: *I can tell you, **Emma**, that your turtle needs antibiotics.* (Emma is the person being addressed.)
>
> No commas: *I can tell that Emma has one sick turtle.* (Emma is being talked about, along with her turtle.)

PUNCTUATE

Add commas as needed to the sentences below. (If a sentence doesn't need a comma, don't add one.)

1. In the event of a flood Florence swim to the cupboard and grab your china.
2. Everybody in French class loved Florence.
3. If you can't stand still Rodney I'll call the sit squad.
4. Thank you Rocky for your minor contribution.
5. I can't believe that Walter sang himself to sleep.
6. If you can't sleep darling drink some warm milk.

WRITE YOUR OWN

Write two sentences that mention a girl named Caroline. In one sentence, directly address Caroline. Make the other sentence about Caroline.

1. _____

   _____

2. _____

   _____

APPOSITIVES

Remember that an appositive is an interrupting element. It interrupts the flow of a sentence to give more information about one of the nouns in the sentence. Here's an example:

Katy saw the dog, **the one with the curly tail**, *and knew she had to have it.*

The one with the curly tail is an appositive that interrupts to give us more information about the dog. That sounds kind of hard, but it isn't. Let's draw a "picture" to illustrate.

First imagine a plain, ordinary sentence. Picture it as a river flowing along, something like this: 〜〜〜〜〜〜〜〜〜〜〜〜〜

Now let's interrupt that flow with an appositive. Think of that river as hitting a couple of rocks and diverting itself for a minute. The commas are the rocks.

〜〜〜〜〜〜〜〜〜〜 **,** appositive **,** 〜〜〜〜〜〜〜〜

PUNCTUATE

Add commas as needed to the sentences below. (If a sentence doesn't need a comma, don't add one.)

1. Punctuation my favorite sport can be dangerous.
2. I was very much afraid of the Abominable Snowman the mysterious creature that supposedly haunts the Northwest until he came to my door selling lightbulbs.
3. Sauerkraut is cabbage with a bad attitude.
4. I will waste tomorrow the best day of the week playing double solitaire with my uncle.
5. Square yo-yos which are popular in Antarctica never really got rolling here in America.
6. The sign the one made entirely of plastic said, "In case of fire, don't throw water on the witch."

WRITE YOUR OWN

Write a sentence that includes an appliance and an appositive.

_____

_____

_____

_____

_____

_____

APPOSITIVES AS SENTENCE BUILDING TOOLS

Sometimes people write oodles and oodles of short sentences that make their writing sound choppy. Appositives can help anyone combine short, choppy sentences into smooth sentences of a variety of lengths. Here's an example.

My brother has been a birdwatcher from birth.
My brother sleeps in a tree house all summer.
*My brother, **a birdwatcher from birth**, sleeps in a tree house all summer.*

PUNCTUATE

Turn each pair of sentences below into one smooth sentence that contains an appositive. Add commas as needed.

1. Mr. Baxter is my pet guppy.

   Mr. Baxter does not like to sleep with the light off.

   _____

2. Ms. Hammersnoot is our camp counselor.

   Ms. Hammersnoot likes to roast marshmallows until they ignite.

   _____

3. Flaming marshmallows are a delicacy in Deadwood.

   Flaming marshmallows are dangerous around porcupines and fireworks.

   _____

4. Ruby is my twelfth cousin.

   By the time Ruby got the new computer out of the box, it was obsolete.

   _____

5. Her new song was released on Tuesday.

   Her new song is already a big hit in New Zealand.

   _____

NECESSARY AND NNECESSARY INTERRUPTERS

Sometimes the words that interrupt the flow of a sentence are not "extras." Sometimes the words are essential to the meaning of the sentence. When the words are necessary to the meaning of the main part of the sentence, you should *not* set the interrupter off with commas. Example:

> *The boy **who wouldn't shave off his goatee** was fired for violating the company policy regarding facial hair.*

In this sentence, the words "who wouldn't shave off his goatee" interrupt the main sentence. However, these words are necessary for the meaning of the sentence. If you leave them out and say simply, "The boy was fired for violating the company policy regarding facial hair," the sentence doesn't have the same meaning. We don't know that it was his attachment to the goatee that resulted in his firing.

However, imagine a slightly different sentence:

> *Jeremy, **who really loved spaghetti and meatballs**, was fired for violating the company policy regarding facial hair.*

This sentence has an interrupter that isn't necessary to the meaning of the sentence. The fact that Jeremy loves spaghetti and meatballs is not essential information. Because it is extra, it is set off with commas.

PUNCTUATE

All of the sentences below have interrupting elements. Some are essential to the meaning of the sentence. Some are not. Put commas around each of the interrupters that are *not* essential to the meaning of the sentence. (If a sentence doesn't need commas, don't add them.)

1. Ellen loved ice cream with chocolate chunks in it and often made a pig of herself at CocoaRama.

2. Skateboarding at the zoo a practice frowned upon by adults can result in some strange and dangerous collisions.

3. The girl who wore a backpack full of candy to school every day often had a sore back.

4. The teacher who had the most boring class in the school didn't even notice when students fell asleep.

5. National Noodle Day which is my favorite holiday is celebrated with piles of piping hot pasta.

A RULE TO REMEMBER

Use commas to separate interrupting elements from the rest of the sentence information.

Interrupting elements break the "flow" of the sentence and give extra or side information. Some common kinds of interrupting elements are:

- phrases or clauses (*His office, **if I remember correctly**, is about ten miles from here.*)

- a name used in a direct address (*I think that you, **Charles**, are my favorite acrobat.*)

- a parenthetical expression: (*You and I, **by the way**, have been elected to bring Melissa to the dance.*)

- an appositive (*Jane, **the woman who fell in love with Tarzan**, loves rhubarb.*)

PUNCTUATE

Add commas as needed to the sentences below. (If a sentence doesn't need a comma, don't add one.)

1. You must my dear friend bring me another one of those delicious stuffed mushrooms.
2. Ethan is by the way the strangest fiddle player who ever waxed a bow.
3. I thought to tell the truth that your dog was a fake.
4. Drop that candy cane Candy and run for your life!
5. If I choose Andrea the fastest runner in school my team will be sure to win.
6. Last week if I recall correctly Mark asked Marlene his boss's daughter for her hand in marriage.
7. The worst thing Sam could imagine other than waking up to see his picture on a milk carton would be a pop quiz in geometry.
8. Right now Anastasia you are the fastest Lego builder in London.
9. Our front yard come to think of it has been the scene of some lovely watermelon fights.
10. You and Mike however are not allowed to participate.

WRITE YOUR OWN

Write three sentences that have something to do with a special promotion at Wal-Mart or Kmart or some other mart. Each sentence must use an interrupter.

1. _____

_____

2. _____

_____

3. _____

_____

QUIZ

PUNCTUATE

Add commas as needed to the sentences below. (If a sentence doesn't need a comma, don't add one.)

1. Hamburger Helper the nation's leading quickie noodle dish has become a favorite of families everywhere.

2. What I can't understand Waldo is why you parked your go-kart directly over the lawn sprinkler.

3. The goldfish America's friendliest kind of fish can live three months in a totally frozen pond.

4. White cobras unlike my cat Denise can go six months without eating a mouse.

5. You by the way are my number one pal!

6. The statues on Easter Island I don't mind saying look exactly like my homeroom teacher.

7. No one looks as beautiful as Veronica does in just a ratty old shirt and blue jeans.

8. Come here Candace and lift this bus off me!

9. My biggest problem if you must know is this pimple on the end of my nose.

10. Chuck on the other hand hates finding *Star Wars* figurines in his cereal box.

WRITE YOUR OWN

Write a paragraph that includes at least three interrupters. Build the paragraph around the subject of potatoes.

_____

_____

_____

_____

_____

_____

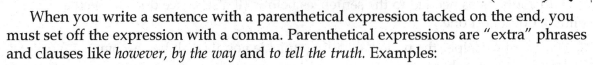

ENDING PARENTHETICAL EXPRESSIONS

When you write a sentence with a parenthetical expression tacked on the end, you must set off the expression with a comma. Parenthetical expressions are "extra" phrases and clauses like *however, by the way* and *to tell the truth*. Examples:

> *You are my fondest memory,* **by the way**.
> *You're the best chicken in the flock,* **in my opinion**.
> *I've left you my matching yo-yos,* **on the other hand**.

PUNCTUATE

Add commas as needed to the sentences below. (If a sentence doesn't need a comma, don't add one.)

1. I'm in love with lobster pie believe it or not.
2. You left your shorts in the laundromat by the way.
3. Billy can have my chair I guess if he promises not to stand on it and blow those awful bubbles.

WRITE YOUR OWN

Write a sentence about a television show. Use an ending parenthetical expression.

_____

_____

_____

_____

_____

_____

ENDING APPOSITIVES

Appositives are phrases and clauses that add more information about a noun (or pronoun) in a sentence. When these appositives appear at the end of a sentence, they are set off by a comma. Examples:

My favorite professor is Dr. Hallaby, **the president of the UFO society.**
Michael is the star quarterback on our football team, **the Rayneville Puppies.**

PUNCTUATE

Add commas as needed to the sentences below. (If a sentence doesn't need a comma, don't add one.)

1. I love watercress soup a nourishing blend of vegetables and water.
2. Do you know Rheba the girl with fantastic vocal cords?
3. My uncle plays the accordion an instrument with a history of happy noises.
4. I am allergic to fur-bearing spaghetti the food that keeps on giving.
5. Jim lives in the attic a place of cobwebs and dreams.

WRITE YOUR OWN

Write a sentence with an appositive at the end. Build the sentence around the subject of "food you might find in the back of the refrigerator."

_____

_____

_____

_____

_____

A RULE TO REMEMBER

Use a comma to separate an ending element from the rest of the sentence.

- An ending element can consist of a person's name, used to show that you are addressing that person. (*I hope you will help me clean out the garage, **Victor**.*)

- An ending element can consist of a parenthetical expression. (*She should be an expert on muskmelons, **at least in my opinion**.*)

- An ending element can consist of an appositive. (*Let me introduce you to Big Brutus, **the leader of our library club**.*)

PUNCTUATE

Add commas as needed to the sentences below. (If a sentence doesn't need a comma, don't add one.)

1. I'm tired of rescuing you Terry.
2. I vote for Tom Turkey the king of gobbledygook.
3. My best friend is this book a tale of young heroes who finally grow up.
4. Tomato ice cream is the best in my opinion.
5. I'm climbing Pikes Peak tomorrow which is the day after Louise gets out of surgery.
6. The *Good Ship Lollipop* has sunk according to reliable sources.
7. My sister lives in Hershey a town of sweet surprises.
8. Stop this tom-foolery immediately Myrtle!
9. Peas taste awful in my opinion.
10. I want a new sister one who is pleasant to have around.

WRITE YOUR OWN

Write three sentences using ending elements. Build the sentences around the subject "snirpwoddles." (Only *you* know what a snirpwoddle is!)

1. _____

_____

2. _____

_____

3. _____

_____

QUIZ

PUNCTUATE

Add commas as needed to the sentences below. (If a sentence doesn't need a comma, don't add one.)

1. I'm sitting here listening to my favorite CD *Rock Around the Hound Dog.*
2. My brother is out on the screened-in porch dozing I think.
3. I like living in our cozy little town Sirloin City.
4. We have more cows here than people I believe.
5. On Saturday nights all the kids go to the Bijou a theater built from scraps of highway pavement.
6. Most of the citizens of Sirloin City are afraid to travel in The Big Apple a code name for New York City.
7. When are we flying to New York City Aunty Willard?
8. You can't leave yet Misty.
9. I left my heart in Holyoke I'd like you to know.
10. I don't care about your heart Margo.

WRITE YOUR OWN

Write three sentences using ending elements. Build the sentences around the subject "music." Be sure to punctuate correctly.

1. _____

_____

_____

2. _____

_____

_____

3. _____

_____

_____

GET SERIES-OUS!

A *television series* is a show that airs week after week. Baseball's World Series refers to several games played to decide the world championship, not just one big game.

A *series* is simply a group of related items arranged one after the other, like a list. The items can be single words or groups of related words (also called *phrases*). The items need to be separated by commas or the words *and* or *or*. * Here's an example:

> *Shawn gets up at 5:00 AM, eats a bowl of Cocoa Puffs, takes a shower and rides a skateboard to school.*

PUNCTUATE

Add commas as needed to the sentences below. (If a sentence doesn't need a comma, don't add one.)

1. My cousin Wolfgang reads sings talks and wiggles his ears while eating.
2. If you leap buildings swim oceans walk tall and smile nicely, they might let you into college some day.
3. Monica entered the jump while you eat contest the smoke detector juggling contest the make an ornament out of noodles contest and the championship frozen pizza toss held in Central Park.

WRITE YOUR OWN

Practice using commas in a series correctly. Choose *three* sentence beginnings from the gray box on the left. Complete each by adding at least three items from the gray box on the right. (You may also make up items of your own to complete the sentences.) Be sure to put commas in the right places. You would not want to experience a nasty visit from the punctuation police!

Sheena admires . . .
Avery always orders . . .
Cassidy considered giving her . . .
Nobody likes . . .
To build a meal you need . . .
Every good party has . . .
I see you like to wear . . .
Please don't bring . . .
You should leave behind all your . . .
Never go on a date with . . .

fake eyebrows • glasses • cabbage
plastic socks • flying monkeys • black lipstick
singing fish • chocolate peanuts • asparagus
brainwaves • geckos • kittens • water wings
the Easter bunny • Elvis • aardvarks
school pictures • lightning • hoola hoops • wigs
pimples • fire alarms • goat cheese
caterpillars • cucumber face cream
octopus omelettes • opera • Oprah • hedgehogs
California • Uruguay • Spandex

* With the last item in a series, you can use a comma before the "and" if you want. In many publications in the United States, that comma is not used any more. Either way is correct.

THE DINKY DOLLAR

In newspaper ads, a writer often wants to describe something as thoroughly as possible without taking up a lot of expensive space. Newspaper ads charge by the amount of space used, so writers like to pack in a lot of words. That means they often use a series of adjectives.

PUNCTUATE

Below are several confusing want ads that use no commas between the adjectives. Add commas so that the items make more sense.

WILL TRADE	GARAGE SALE TOMORROW	FOR RENT IN THE CITY
Have moody adventurous well-trained talented aardvark to trade for gas grill or large stand-up hairdryer. Can't wait to meet you! Drop by at 345 South Dimwood Avenue, evenings.	Selling brownies watch cordless phone wire snips car radio sneaker laces computer printer cable printer hot dog maker bicycle tire pump handle for lawn mower blade sharpener and ant farm.	Small cozy cheap no frills fragrant windowless apartment above Spanky's Garage on 103rd Street. $590/mo. Call 555-3334.

WRITE YOUR OWN

Now write three ads of your own for the Dinky Dollar, each ad including a series of adjectives that describe something that is for sale.

A RULE TO REMEMBER

Use commas to separate items in a series.

PUNCTUATE

Add commas as needed to the sentences below. (If a sentence doesn't need a comma, don't add one.)

1. He used to be good at golf good at tennis and good at being a nagging menace.
2. She used the phone to call her mother to call her boyfriend and to scratch a little itchy spot in the middle of her back.
3. Desmond hates sauerkraut pancakes onions mussels and mint-flavored salami.
4. Nobody knows if you are lying pretending exaggerating prevaricating or just kidding.
5. Jungles are hot noisy sweaty wet dangerous places with no decent theme parks.
6. On my last trip to Australia, I boxed with a kangaroo trained a dingo to fetch swam with a platypus and came home with a chunk of the Great Barrier Reef lodged in my foot.
7. Nobody trains a chimp buys it new clothes teaches it to read recipes and then sends it off to cooking school without a hand-carved spatula!
8. If anybody cared about my feelings worried about my worries or shared my joys pains hopes and fears, then maybe I wouldn't want to move all the way to New Guinea in the fall.

WRITE YOUR OWN

Write a sentence of your own that includes items in a series. Make it a sentence about standing in the school lunch line staring at the entrees on the stainless steel table in front of you.

_____

_____

_____

_____

_____

_____

QUIZ

PUNCTUATE

Add commas as needed to the sentences below. (If a sentence doesn't need a comma, don't add one.)

1. Ben's favorite breakfast is cold pizza grape juice Froot Loops and a banana.
2. At the yard sale, Melody found a fencing sword an hourglass a huge pine cone Christmas tree and three plastic bull fighters.
3. Joel used soup cans plastic spoons a bicycle chain aluminum foil and orange suspenders to make a self-propelled toaster.
4. Rice cakes can be used as a source of carbohydrates as coasters for paper cups as life rafts for hamsters and as earrings to go with "big" hair.
5. If I had a million dollars, I would buy a pizza factory rent an island for a month hire a butler to wait on me and send my big sister away to boarding school.
6. Mark went to Chicago to learn basket weaving cat grooming ear piercing and worm management.
7. Dorothy hates flying mammals loves clicking her heels dislikes high winds mistrusts talking trees and enjoys a good bowl of chicken salad with parsley.
8. If I lived on an island, I would send messages in bottles eat turtle burgers sleep in a palm tree and drink coconut milk three times a day.
9. I can't believe you told Marcy about my dog my cat my mother my fish and my false teeth!
10. Don't miss the exciting exhilarating mystifying and amazingly brilliant new film called *The Broccoli Murders*.

WRITE YOUR OWN

Write a sentence of your own that includes a series and mentions something with four legs.

_____

_____

_____

_____

_____

FORS AND NORS AND SUCH

A comma is needed when the word *and, but, or, for, nor* or *yet* connects two complete sentences—in other words, in a compound sentence. You might as well memorize the connecting words (also called conjunctions) that need commas when used in a compound sentence:

> *And*
> *But*
> *Or*
> *For*
> *Nor*
> *Yet*

Make a chant of them. Set them to a tune. If you take a few moments to memorize them, a lot of punctuation problems that come up later on will be easier.

PUNCTUATE

Add commas as needed to the sentences below. (If a sentence doesn't need a comma, don't add one.) Remember: You need a comma with the connecting words above only if they connect complete sentences.

1. Last year I was a space alien in a Christmas play but this year I'm an ornament.
2. Marvin hated vitamins for his mother always made him take them with a liver milkshake.
3. Kate weaseled out of the bake sale yet I still think she would make a great leader for our Ducks Anonymous meeting.
4. Mel's mother raises geckos but refuses to cook them.
5. Elizabeth absolutely loves peanut butter and pickle sandwiches but she won't touch any other kind of sandwich in the world.

WRITE YOUR OWN

Write three compound sentences. Build the sentences around the subject "The Mysterious Noise."

1. _____

_____

2. _____

_____

3. _____

_____

COMMAS AND COMPOUNDS

Use a comma with the connecting word *and, but, or, for, nor* or *yet* when it connects two independent clauses—in other words, when it connects two sentences that could stand alone. Examples:

Yes: *I'll trade you my computer for your motorcycle, **or** you can have what's behind locker number three.*

No: *I'll trade you my computer for your motorcycle or your tent.*

PUNCTUATE

Add commas as needed to the sentences below. (If a sentence doesn't need a comma, don't add one.)

1. Al pushed a cucumber off the roof but it bounced off a baby carriage and landed on a dachshund.
2. I do not believe in Munchkins nor do I think they can dance in real life.
3. Nobody saw the car coming and no one tried to warn the poor pigeon trying to cross the street.
4. People laughed and shouted at her as they drove by but Jennifer cheerfully kept rinsing the giraffe.
5. She is not against fast food nor is she in favor of the slow stuff.

WRITE YOUR OWN

Write a paragraph that includes at least three compound sentences. Use the subject, "Was that a martian or what?"

_____

_____

_____

_____

_____

_____

A RULE TO REMEMBER

Use a comma —
along with the connecting words
and, but, or, for, nor or *yet* —
to separate the two parts
of a compound sentence.

PUNCTUATE

Add commas as needed to the sentences below. (If a sentence doesn't need a comma, don't add one.)

1. I'm about to say goodbye to the city where I was born and raised and I won't miss it a bit.

2. Nobody can make a chocolate shake or an oatmeal-raisin cookie like Kent but I would sure like to try after I take that cooking class I signed up for.

3. I'm all for sports and entertainment and goofing off but you haven't got a chance with that stupid chicken-racing scheme!

4. You may cheerfully eat the cauliflower and tuna sandwich I served you or you can sit quietly and eat nothing at all.

5. By the way, students may not wear boots in the gym nor may they ride bikes in the bathroom.

WRITE YOUR OWN

Write three compound sentences of your own about cats.

1. _____

_____

_____

2. _____

_____

_____

3. _____

_____

_____

QUIZ

PUNCTUATE

Add commas as needed to the sentences below. (If a sentence doesn't need a comma, don't add one.)

1. You can mail the application to the address at the top of the instruction sheet or you can use your computer to fill out an on-line application.

2. Dr. Shawna McCoy graduated from Harvard with a degree in medicine but one day she decided to give up her medical practice and become a jockey!

3. My sister and I spent seven hours shopping at the mall on Saturday yet we couldn't find anything that seemed quite right for Dad's birthday present.

4. Jessica couldn't see why her mother had to be so unreasonable about her weekend curfew nor could she see why her father had to be so unreasonable and agree with her mother about it.

5. Ed loved sailing more than just about anything else in the universe yet he lived half a continent away from an ocean.

WRITE YOUR OWN

Write three compound sentences about any subject that begins with the letter "s."

1. _____

_____

2. _____

_____

3. _____

_____

DATES, ADDRESSES AND TITLES

PUNCTUATE

Add commas as needed to the sentences below. (If a sentence doesn't need a comma, don't add one.) Remember to use commas to separate the different parts of a date or an address.

1. The twins were born on July 13 1987 in the hospital at 45601 Mulberry Street Hereford, Colorado 80732.

2. Brian Stile Jr. cut a new album on November 14 1998 in Nashville Tennessee.

3. On August 4 1991 Barry Almaretto Ph.D. had the first brilliant original idea of his life.

4. On the morning of September 12 1994 the house at 123456 Whelton Drive Hillville Idaho was picked up by a twister and set down again somewhere in Montana.

5. I lived at 340 West Pile Street Newark Alabama before I started sleeping at the cheese factory.

6. Dear Madeline

     Will you marry me? If not, will you at least go out to dinner with me?

   Love
   Ted

WRITE YOUR OWN

Write a sentence that includes a date and an address and something that smells wonderful.

_____

_____

_____

_____

_____

_____

QUIZ

PUNCTUATE

Add commas as needed to the sentences below. (If a sentence doesn't need a comma, don't add one.)

1. Candace Cornflower D.V.M. spends a lot of time at her animal clinic designing diets for overweight condors.

2. On October 4 1942 Malcolm's grandparents built a house on the ranch at 2214 Highway 184 Kelby New Jersey 08888.

3. Dear Will

   I am all alone in the apartment since you and Jasper moved out. I think I like it a lot better.

   Sincerely

   Hector

4. If you could travel ahead to September 14 4078 would you bring your MP3 player or a thermos full of Gatorade?

5. Melvin Schwinnbaum Jr. is in charge of the talent show this year.

WRITE YOUR OWN

Write a short letter that invites someone to attend a party. Be sure to include the complete date and address of the party.

_____

_____

_____

_____

_____

_____

COORDINATE ADJECTIVES

When two or more adjectives come right before a noun, the adjectives are often separated by commas. How do you tell if the comma is needed? Try substituting the word *and* between the adjectives. If the result sounds natural, use a comma. If it does not, leave the comma out. Examples:

No comma needed: *The winner is the little brown dog.*
(The winner is the little and brown dog? No.)
Comma needed: *The boring, conceited candidate won the election.*
(The boring and conceited candidate? Yes.)

PUNCTUATE

Add commas as needed to the sentences below. (If a sentence doesn't need a comma, don't add one.)

1. The little black kitten sat on a mitten.
2. Black and blue marks lined the top of his cranium.
3. Old nasty bread crumbs are better than no crumbs.
4. Even with her tall beautiful sister beside her, Anna was outstanding in a crowd.
5. I once lived in an ancient leaky hut in the middle of Borneo.
6. Keep your dark and dangerous eyes to yourself.
7. He was in an aging crippled car when it sailed off into the lake.
8. Black and white stop signs lined the roads of the strange city.
9. Only eager energetic candidates have a chance at becoming President.
10. Without a cold hard look at the facts, I can't make a decent decision.

WRITE YOUR OWN

Write a sentence that describes a movie or a book. Use two or more adjectives, side by side, in the sentence.

_____

_____

_____

_____

_____

QUIZ

PUNCTUATE

Add commas as needed to the sentences below. (If a sentence doesn't need a comma, don't add one.) Remember to use a comma to separate coordinate adjectives that come before a noun.

1. The long hard road to success is traveled by many soles.
2. The dark terrifying mansion was the only building we could see for miles.
3. If you like chicken nuggets, you'll like these sweet spicy balls of broccoli.
4. What really matters is that you become an intelligent hardworking postman.
5. You can't go to the movies in that lopsided ridiculous hat.

WRITE YOUR OWN

Write three sentences of your own about a time when you had a babysitter that drove you crazy. (Or you can write about a time when you were the babysitter at a house full of strange, annoying children.) Make sure you use at least two adjectives, side by side, in each sentence.

1. _____

_____

2. _____

_____

3. _____

_____

CUMULATIVE REVIEWS AND TEST

REVIEW

PUNCTUATE

Add commas as needed to the sentences below. (If a sentence doesn't need a comma, don't add one.)

1. By the time Abe got there which was well after midnight the ape was gone.
2. Frankly Frank I don't care if you're the slowest rat in the race.
3. Finding flies catching flies and eating flies is a frog's favorite after-school activity.
4. The circus I'll have you know is a perfect place to go for a tightrope experience.
5. On August 4 1991 Sam Benham had the first brilliant inspirational idea of his life.
6. Rodney watch out for that tea cup!
7. A person should never loan money to a relative in my opinion.
8. Of all the roller rinks in the world Angela Bernice Andrea Sabrina Melissa and Ramona had to walk into mine.
9. Delores likes peanuts more than anything.
10. Antonio because of his size almost emptied the pool when he did a belly flop.
11. By coming together like this and learning to put up with each other we learn to be better Boy Scouts.
12. I'm going to a wild west camp this summer but I am not allowed to bring a camera to record the misery.
13. You will be able to produce your own bagel-making video when you get enough time when you get enough money and when you get enough courage.
14. Los Angeles the "City of Angels" contains movie stars artists dancers singers playwrights and the footprints of that little mischievous alien E.T.
15. To tell the truth I don't really care for Uncle Tim's barbecued tuna burgers.
16. For a refund on Wasted Watermelon concert tickets write to Horace Townsend at 33522 River Muck Way Heartache Alabama 36543
17. Dear Dad

    Please send me some money. Pretty please.

    Your loving son

    David
18. I had a long weary agonizing wait in the dreary office of Wilma Hipple M.D.
19. Mrs. Bender gave her son two tickets to see a Norwegian comic opera the one called *The Valiant Snow People.*
20. I'm not a psychiatrist or a doctor but let me give you some advice Mario.

WRITE YOUR OWN

Write a paragraph that includes at least five commas used correctly. Build your sentences around the subject of an annoying salesperson who has come to the door selling used appliances.

REVIEW

PUNCTUATE

Add commas as needed to the sentences below. (If a sentence doesn't need a comma, don't add one.)

1. Yes Lynette hates beef cheese carrots and anything green at least when she eats at home.
2. Chauncy don't you know what a chifforobe is?
3. The Pillsbury Dough Boy the Munchkins the Seven Dwarfs and my friend Teresa are all famous for being shorter than a coffee table.
4. Incidentally I want you to bring me the fly swatter.
5. Dear Madeline

   In your last letter you insulted my dog threatened my cat and lied about the dent in my car. Don't write again.

   Angrily

   Meredith
6. Incidentally when are you going to have a good long serious look at the junk on your back porch Aunt Eunice?
7. Because insects have grown immune to many bug sprays that are on the market all over the world today people have been relying on flytraps.
8. Here are some flowers my little pumpkin for your birthday.
9. Before my mother could get to him he was bound up like a mummy.
10. Before you came into my life with your wonderful gooseberry dumplings I could never gain any weight Pierre.
11. Nobody believed Clarissa when she announced that March 3 1094 was an important day in history but she went on to prove that she was right with two books and a magazine article.
12. You can call me Fred or Jed or Ned or Ted or nothing at all Melissa.
13. Your brother incidentally got married last night in Reno.
14. Alvin always an innocent bystander was run over by a wandering woman with a shopping cart.
15. Nobody but Wally Thomas Jr. my unusual next-door neighbor can eat a pizza underwater.
16. All of Santa's letters were mistakenly sent to 1689 Rutemeyer Street Anchorage Alaska 99543.
17. I won't eat peas however.
18. I can't believe you or your mother or your father didn't recognize Grandma's parrot the green and red one named Bilbo.

TEST

PUNCTUATE

Add commas as needed to the sentences below. (If a sentence doesn't need a comma, don't add one.)

1. He was broken down weary and tired of pre-school.
2. Nobody keeps lettuce crispier and greener than Edith Tupperware my grandmother.
3. The boss wants Daniel to wash the windows on the thirty-third floor.
4. If you want a ride to the mall this evening you had better help me with these dishes.
5. Everybody in town over 60 years old is at the town's biggest celebration the Librarians' Overdue Dance.
6. Nobody in school nobody at home and nobody in the chess club knew that I had joined the bell choir.
7. Oliver I thought I might mail you some dental floss.
8. If you do every single page of your math homework every night and pass all the remaining tests with at least 99% you might still manage to pass the class.
9. Kristina and Carleta to tell you the truth aren't the ones I would pick to win.
10. For your own good if you'll just exercise eat right sleep tight and wash your fruit you will live a long and healthy life.
11. If all goes well you should be in Madagascar by morning Brett.
12. You are a healthy vibrant young bunny yet I see a weakness in your hopping technique Ernest.
13. A pink cloud hung in the sky above the crowd watching the championship soccer match and it stayed there throughout the game.
14. Emily Rodder M.D. and Frank Wall Ph.D. decided to quit their jobs and set up a Go-Kart track at 6793 Kingston Drive Waterhole Mississippi 38681.
15. I kept falling asleep while we read that raggedy boring book about Sir Chuck who was some kind of knight.
16. Cara don't torment your little brother.
17. Ashley was exhausted by the time she left the pound incidentally.
18. His sister the one who lived at 3409 Bruiser Lane Handown Ohio threw him a "new idea" party and invited all his old rich annoying friends including Charles Oldhow M.D.
19. Dear Ms. Zesbaugh

    Please excuse my absence. I stayed home because I felt so good today.
    Your student
    Alissa
20. Sarah didn't want to wear the mustard-colored cardigan her sister had knitted for her and she also didn't feel much like putting on the pink skirt her mother had made to go with it.

ANSWER KEYS

ANSWER KEYS

ANSWER KEY, PAGE 9, FIRST THINGS FIRST
Punctuate

1. Well, I for one do not know any stand-up librarians.
2. Sadly, he took his bassoon and went home.
3. No, there's nothing wrong with Aunt Louise.

Write Your Own
Answers will vary. Here are a few possibilities.

1. Reluctantly, I wore the buffalo costume to the masquerade ball.
2. Amazingly, Tim traded his Cal Ripken baseball card for my goldfish.

ANSWER KEY, PAGE 10, SHORT STUFF
Punctuate

1. Oddly enough, I've grown fond of milk toast.
2. Practically speaking, I wouldn't own a blender if my life depended on it.
3. Although he denies it, I'm not at all surprised that Paul ate your Jell-O.

Write Your Own
Answers will vary. Here are a few possibilities.

1. Just for kicks, I made a broccoli milkshake.
2. Strangely enough, it was delicious.

ANSWER KEY, PAGE 11, LONG STUFF
Punctuate

1. If you ever have a chance to meet my parakeet, skip it.
2. While we watched Allison lunge for the aquarium that was about to topple off the table, we all held our breath.
3. In the event of a worldwide lettuce shortage, eat cabbage.

Write Your Own
Answers will vary. Here are a few possibilities.

1. If you really must know, I love oatmeal pie.
2. After Belinda works the night shift at Kwik-E-Mart, she sleeps past noon.
3. Because Bill already owns rollerblades, a skateboard would make a great gift.

ANSWER KEY, PAGE 13, INTERRUPTERS
Punctuate

1. No one in the school, however, knew that Bill's middle name was "Noodles."
2. The *Titanic*, an unsinkable ship, sank.
3. My brother thinks that cauliflower, the world's friendliest vegetable, goes well with chocolate sauce.
4. Mrs. Gymtoe, after being hypnotized by Professor Drool during an assembly, fell off the stage into a pile of seventh graders.
5. The most important thing the astronauts took to the moon, not counting a ton of powdered vegetables, was a shiny roll of duct tape.

Write Your Own
Answers will vary. Here is one possibility.

Last night, after everyone was asleep, a flying saucer landed between my house and the Taco Bell next door. I was terrified that the ship's aliens, big green blobs with fangs, were going to kidnap and eat me. It turns out, however, they just wanted some 39¢ burritos from Taco Bell.

ANSWER KEY, PAGE 15, ENDING STUFF
Punctuate

1. You are my fondest memory, by the way.
2. I must have that lobster in the window, the one with the sumptuous tail.
3. I never expected you to tell everyone, Harvey.
4. You can't go to the movies in that ridiculous outfit, Melanie.
5. I like ridiculous outfits, Mom.

Write Your Own
Answers will vary. Here is one possibility.

Karen is the most annoying neighbor in the world, by the way. She is always singing old disco tunes at the top of her lungs, which makes me grit my teeth. Sometimes Karen even dances to her singing, making me want to scream.

Answer Keys

Punctuate

1. Max is clever, wise, wonderfully funny and good with gorillas.
2. Uncle Farley is rich, weird, whiny and handy with a plunger.
3. Maria used her babysitting money to buy face powder, bubble gum, fly spray and Oreos.

Write Your Own
Answers will vary. Here are a few possibilities.

1. Chris has a sports equipment box filled with two tennis rackets, a soccer ball, a bowling ball and a kick board.
2. Everyone likes Liz because she makes the best lemon bread, strawberry Jell-O mold and marble cheesecake.

ANSWER KEY, PAGE 19, COMPOUNDS
Punctuate

1. Turkeys are not exactly known for their great brain power, and nobody thinks that worms are likely to win scholarships to Harvard.
2. He hated television and music, but he loved doing algebra equations more than anything on Earth.
3. Mary and Joe went on a hike up the Absolom Canyon on a beautiful fall day.

Write Your Own
Answers will vary. Here are a few possibilities.

1. Kyle and I starting throwing tomatoes when we ran out of water balloons, and they worked much better.
2. The drive to Yellowstone was very pretty, but we sure had lots of bug guts on our windshield by the time we got there.

ANSWER KEY, PAGE 21, DATES
Punctuate

1. On December 4, 1289, a Roman teenager invented the world's first dating service.
2. Years ago on November 1, 1988, Elvira Twang decided that by January 12, 2044, she would have her own hypnotist's shop in downtown Potato Springs.
3. When the mud races began on June 4, 1995, Edna was ready with self-cleaning eyeglasses.
4. It was early on the morning of May 5, 1888, that Alfred J. Oops learned the meaning of the concept "hazardous waste."
5. At midnight on August 13, 1957, Alvin Andrews dreamed of frozen cabbage burgers.

Write Your Own
Answers will vary. Here are a few possibilities.

1. On August 31, 1998, I finally got my braces off.
2. I'll never forget May 14, 1999, because Bernard finally agreed to go to the movies with me.

ANSWER KEY, PAGE 23, ADDRESSES
Punctuate

1. Send your complaints to Mary Snookum, 141 Peewee Drive, Hickory, Arkansas 72065.
2. Please send my refund to 6543 Hullabaloo Lane, Fort Almost, Texas 78514.
3. No one can tell the future except the Snapple salesman who lives at 44321 Anxious Avenue, Mystic, Florida 34221.
4. If your zeppelin lands a little early, stop by and see me at 99887 Elbow Lane, Loosejaw, Alaska 99604.

Write Your Own
Answers will vary. Here are a few possibilities.

1. LaVerne has a big crush on Robert, so we always have to drive by his house at 1434 Edison Avenue, LaJunta, Colorado 81050.
2. Every Saturday morning we eat breakfast at the Garden Creek Cafe at 236 North Center Street, Wholesome, Wisconsin 65236.

ANSWER KEY, PAGE 25, JR., SR. AND TITLES
Punctuate

1. Otto Rizzuto, Jr., has discovered that the number of people who die from meatloaf overdose equals the number of people who work for Wal-Mart but actually shop at Kmart.

2. For Teacher of the Year, I recommend Archie Sprinkler, Ed.D., for his contribution to wood shop technology and the invention of decorative flowers made from used hamburger wrappers.
3. Sergeant Emily Strong, R.N., is the best nurse in Company D.
4. Before you throw her off the flying insect committee, let it be known that Imelda Johnson, Ph.D, was the first to make anti-mosquito powder from dried clam shells.
5. Nobody knows how much work Axel Backfill, Ph.D., put into the invention of spray toothpaste.

Write Your Own
Answers will vary. Here are a few possibilities.

1. After Seymour Fendlehessy, Jr., was born, the Fendlehessy poodle had to sleep outside.
2. My cousin Flo brought her new boyfriend, Milton Garcia, M.D., to Thanksgiving dinner just to impress my Grandpa Roy.

Answer Key, page 27, Letters
Punctuate

#1:

Dear darling mice,

I'm sorry about your missing tails. My wife went a little crazy when she got her credit card bill for a new set of steak knives, and you just happened to get in the way. I have a brother in Sausalito who is a plastic surgeon. He would be happy to reconstruct your tails. Please contact him at 778-777-8891. He only works on Saturday.
Sincerely,
Farmer Hopkins

#2:

Dear Cinderella,

We miss you terribly. We spent so many joyful hours watching you clean the fireplace ashes and dust under our beds. Please accept our apology for any dirt we may have caused you to get under your fingernails. Mother would like to see your castle, and if you would invite us to the next ball, we would bring you some turnip cookies. Kiss the prince for us since we will never get to.

Love,
Your two stepsisters and Ma

#3:

Dear Cable-O-Rama President:

Please cancel my cable television subscription. I am very dissatisfied with your service and can't take it anymore.
Sincerely,
Raynelda Murphy

Answer Key, page 29, Side by Side
Punctuate

1. Nobody saw the rumpled, lonely pigeon sitting on the statue's nose.
2. It was a dark and stormy night.
3. Nobody believed his weary, pointless lies.
4. The lonely and dejected slug sat on a soggy bun.
5. Jeff ate an attractive, steamy bowl of Spam nuggets.

Write Your Own
Answers will vary. Here are a few possibilities.

1. Corned beef and cabbage make a surprisingly delicious and satisfying pizza.
2. I can never eat pizza again after throwing up the disgusting, smelly pizza from Pizza Smorgasbord.

Answer Key, page 32, Addressing Directly
Punctuate

1. Mom, could I please have more of that delicious broccoli and oyster casserole?
2. Linda wants to exchange her brothers for some new ones.
3. Linda wants a new fur-lined lunch box for her birthday.
4. Linda, get over here and wash this turtle!
5. Ira, don't you want to dance at the bar mitzvah?

ANSWER KEYS

Write Your Own

Answers will vary. Here are a few possibilities.

1. Alex, your hamster is adorable.
2. Alex won't let anyone else pet his new hamster.

ANSWER KEY, PAGE 33, PARENTHETICALLY SPEAKING
Punctuate

1. To tell you the truth, I've learned more from my grandpa than anyone.
2. On second thought, I've learned a lot from my pet hamster, Richard.
3. In my opinion, he's a tough little rodent.
4. In short, I'm thrilled with his performance on the XK3000 Whirler Coaster.
5. In fact, once he starts spinning, the fur really flies.

Write Your Own

Answers will vary. Here is one possibility.

In my opinion, no food on earth tastes better than a biscuit from Kentucky Fried Chicken.

ANSWER KEY, PAGE 34, LONG AND SHORT OF IT
Punctuate

1. When you think about it, decimals are just periods with a math education.
2. Of all the scientific principles around today, I like gravity the best.
3. Beans with red sauce are better than corn dogs on a stick.
4. I can't believe you're the only person in the park with a piccolo.
5. After sneaking into the house later than he should have and being pretty sure his parents hadn't woken up, Chuck accidentally kicked the cat.

Write Your Own

Answers will vary. Here are a few possibilities.

1. When you eat cake with licorice frosting, your tongue turns a funky shade of black.
2. Since you seem to like the color beige so much, I crocheted you an afghan using three different beige yarns.

ANSWER KEY, PAGE 35, REVIEW
Punctuate

1. Thinking back, I would say that Harold was too close to the edge.
2. Tyrone, just call her and ask her.
3. Oh, I can't wait to bake you some Spam muffins!
4. In the future, keep your cuckoo in the closet.
5. By the way, you left your little brother at the car wash.
6. If you want, I could fix you some creamed turnips.
7. Peter picked a peck of pickled peppers.
8. While under the boardwalk, he found Waldo's retainer.

Write Your Own

Answers will vary. Here are a few possibilities.

1. Unfortunately, Molly is a terrible hunting dog because she is in love with a buck elk.
2. Interestingly enough, my cat let me paint her claws a nice shade of raspberry.
3. Before the thieves could take anything, the Livingston's pet goat chased them away.
4. Believe it or not, Abigail's goldfish likes to drink Mountain Dew.

ANSWER KEY, PAGE 36, QUIZ
Punctuate

1. After I finish a wrestling match, I like to sit down with a Twinkie and a quart of Kool-Aid.
2. When I first got started in wrestling, I couldn't get a good grip on their snouts.
3. Before my career took off, I used to wait tables in Louie's Lizard Lounge, shine shoes at the Algonquin Hotel and play the accordion for tips in the subway station.
4. When I have free time, I like to go shopping for alligator ties, alligator boots and alligator wallets.
5. If I had it to do all over again, I would forget alligator wrestling and become an encyclopedia salesman, a used car salesman or maybe an English teacher.
6. Alligators aren't all that smart.
7. Because I have become famous, every alligator from here to Africa wants to wrestle me.

8. No, I never eat alligator stew.
9. Mary, I don't think you should eat alligator stew either.
10. By the way, I don't think anyone should eat alligator stew.

Write Your Own
Answers will vary. Here are a few possibilities.

1. After everything is said and done, do you really like wearing alligator loafers, or are you just being mean?
2. Melvin, have you ever seen an alligator cry crocodile tears?
3. Generally speaking, don't women usually make better alligator wrestlers?

ANSWER KEY, PAGE 37, PARENTHETICAL EXPRESSIONS
Punctuate

1. Nobody in our class, in my opinion, is a match for Burnell Beetlebaum.
2. Nobody except Marlene, to tell you the truth, can eat 14 sub sandwiches while riding a pogo stick.
3. It seems strange, on the other hand, that Marlene even owns a pogo stick.
4. I can't, of course, go with you to the Mushroom Festival.
5. I can't believe, even if I wanted to, that you're guilty of grand chocolate theft.
6. No one, in my opinion, should believe her story about the flying fur ball!

Write Your Own
Answers will vary. Here is one possibility.

I've never eaten anything so delicious, after all, as Dixie's pigeon casserole.

ANSWER KEY, PAGE 38, DIRECT ADDRESS
Punctuate

1. In the event of a flood, Florence, swim to the cupboard and grab your china.
2. Everybody in French class loved Florence.
3. If you can't stand still, Rodney, I'll call the sit squad.
4. Thank you, Rocky, for your minor contribution.

5. I can't believe that Walter sang himself to sleep.
6. If you can't sleep, darling, drink some warm milk.

Write Your Own
Answers will vary. Here are a few possibilities.

1. I must admit, Caroline, I don't like you at all.
2. Caroline is mean and bossy.

ANSWER KEY, PAGE 39, APPOSITIVES
Punctuate

1. Punctuation, my favorite sport, can be dangerous.
2. I was very much afraid of the Abominable Snowman, the mysterious creature that supposedly haunts the Northwest, until he came to my door selling lightbulbs.
3. Sauerkraut is cabbage with a bad attitude.
4. I will waste tomorrow, the best day of the week, playing double solitaire with my uncle.
5. Square yo-yos, which are popular in Antarctica, never really got rolling here in America.
6. The sign, the one made entirely of plastic, said, "In case of fire, don't throw water on the witch."

Write Your Own
Answers will vary. Here is one possibility.

Brenda stocks her refrigerator, the tiny one in her room, with nothing but grape Kool-Aid.

ANSWER KEY, PAGE 40, APPOSITIVES AS SENTENCE BUILDING TOOLS
Punctuate

1. Mr. Baxter, my pet guppy, does not like to sleep with the light off.
2. Ms. Hammersnoot, our camp counselor, likes to roast marshmallows until they ignite.
3. Flaming marshmallows, a delicacy in Deadwood, are dangerous around porcupines and fireworks.
4. By the time Ruby, my twelfth cousin, got the new computer out of the box, it was obsolete.
5. Her new song, already a big hit in New Zealand, was released on Tuesday.

Answer Keys

ANSWER KEY, PAGE 41, NECESSARY AND UNNECESSARY INTERRUPTERS

Punctuate

1. Ellen loved ice cream with chocolate chunks in it and often made a pig of herself at CocoaRama.
2. Skateboarding at the zoo, a practice frowned upon by adults, can result in some strange and dangerous collisions.
3. The girl who wore a backpack full of candy to school every day often had a sore back.
4. The teacher who had the most boring class in the school didn't even notice when students fell asleep.
5. National Noodle Day, which is my favorite holiday, is celebrated with piles of piping hot pasta.

ANSWER KEY, PAGE 42, REVIEW

Punctuate

1. You must, my dear friend, bring me another one of those delicious stuffed mushrooms.
2. Ethan is, by the way, the strangest fiddle player who ever waxed a bow.
3. I thought, to tell the truth, that your dog was a fake.
4. Drop that candy cane, Candy, and run for your life!
5. If I choose Andrea, the fastest runner in school, my team will be sure to win.
6. Last week, if I recall correctly, Mark asked Marlene, his boss's daughter, for her hand in marriage.
7. The worst thing Sam could imagine, other than waking up to see his picture on a milk carton, would be a pop quiz in geometry.
8. Right now, Anastasia, you are the fastest Lego builder in London.
9. Our front yard, come to think of it, has been the scene of some lovely watermelon fights.
10. You and Mike, however, are not allowed to participate.

Write Your Own

Answers will vary. Here are a few possibilities.

1. We have to get to K-Mart, the one on Riverside Avenue, first thing in the morning because they are having a sale on magenta house paint.
2. Wal-Mart, if I remember correctly, is holding a sale on wart remover.
3. K-Mart, unbelievably, is promoting guppies that live more than six weeks, guaranteed.

ANSWER KEY, PAGE 43, QUIZ

Punctuate

1. Hamburger Helper, the nation's leading quickie noodle dish, has become a favorite of families everywhere.
2. What I can't understand, Waldo, is why you parked your go-kart directly over the lawn sprinkler.
3. The goldfish, America's friendliest kind of fish, can live three months in a totally frozen pond.
4. White cobras, unlike my cat Denise, can go six months without eating a mouse.
5. You, by the way, are my number one pal!
6. The statues at Easter Island, I don't mind saying, look exactly like my homeroom teacher.
7. No one looks as beautiful as Veronica does in just a ratty old shirt and blue jeans.
8. Come here, Candace, and lift this bus off me!
9. My biggest problem, if you must know, is this pimple on the end of my nose.
10. Chuck, on the other hand, hates finding *Star Wars* figurines in his cereal box.

Write Your Own

Answers will vary. Here is one possibility.

Helen, Martha's grandma, warned me to never, ever, ever eat a baked potato in Montana. I was truly puzzled by Helen, usually an extremely quiet woman, making such a strong statement. So I asked her, "Why on earth, Helen, should I never, ever eat a baked potato in Montana?" She explained, rather matter-of-factly, that they don't serve a decent-sized potato in Montana, and you can never get one with bacon bits and sour cream.

ANSWER KEYS

Answer Key, page 44, Ending Parenthetical Phrases
Punctuate

1. I'm in love with lobster pie, believe it or not.
2. You left your shorts in the laundromat, by the way.
3. Billy can have my chair, I guess, if he promises not to stand on it and blow those awful bubbles.

Write Your Own
Answers will vary. Here is one possibility.

I still secretly watch *Mister Rogers' Neighborhood*, believe it or not.

Answer Key, page 45, Ending Appositives
Punctuate

1. I love watercress soup, a nourishing blend of vegetables and water.
2. Do you know Rheba, the girl with fantastic vocal cords?
3. My uncle plays the accordion, an instrument with a history of happy noises.
4. I am allergic to fur-bearing spaghetti, the food that keeps on giving.
5. Jim lives in the attic, a place of cobwebs and dreams.

Write Your Own
Answers will vary. Here is one possibility.

Rather than wash out the six-month-old tater tots, I threw away the entire container, the yellow tupperware with a lid.

Answer Key, page 46, Review
Punctuate

1. I'm tired of rescuing you, Terry.
2. I vote for Tom Turkey, the king of gobbledygook.
3. My best friend is this book, a tale of young heroes who finally grow up.
4. Tomato ice cream is the best, in my opinion.
5. I'm climbing Pikes Peak tomorrow, which is the day after Louise gets out of surgery.
6. The *Good Ship Lollipop* has sunk, according to reliable sources.

7. My sister lives in Hershey, a town of sweet surprises.
8. Stop this tom-foolery immediately, Myrtle!
9. Peas taste awful, in my opinion.
10. I want a new sister, one who is pleasant to have around.

Write Your Own
Answers will vary. Here are a few possibilities.

1. Ellie washes her sheets every other day for fear of snirpwoddles, also called bedbugs.
2. Ellie says that more than a million snirpwoddles live in people's beds and they gnaw on our elbows, believe it or not.
3. She sure is paranoid, in my opinion.

Answer Key, page 47, Quiz
Punctuate

1. I'm sitting here listening to my favorite CD, *Rock Around the Hound Dog*.
2. My brother is out on the screened-in porch dozing, I think.
3. I like living in our cozy little town, Sirloin City.
4. We have more cows here than people, I believe.
5. On Saturday nights all the kids go to the Bijou, a theater built from scraps of highway pavement.
6. Most of the citizens of Sirloin City are afraid to travel in The Big Apple, a code name for New York City.
7. When are we flying to New York City, Aunty Willard?
8. You can't leave yet, Misty.
9. I left my heart in Holyoke, I'd like you to know.
10. I don't care about your heart, Margo.

Write Your Own
Answers will vary. Here are a few possibilities.

1. My favorite kind of music is yodeling, I must admit.
2. I took yodeling lessons from Mrs. Wolfenbarger, the old Austrian woman down the street.
3. You can always borrow *Yo-Yo-Yodeling*, my favorite CD.

ANSWER KEY, PAGE 48, GET SERIES-OUS
Punctuate

1. My cousin Wolfgang reads, sings, talks and wiggles his ears while eating.
2. If you leap buildings, swim oceans, walk tall and smile nicely, they might let you into college some day.
3. Monica entered the jump while you eat contest, the smoke detector juggling contest, the make an ornament out of noodles contest and the championship frozen pizza toss held in Central Park.

Write Your Own
Answers will vary. Here are a few possibilities.

1. Cassidy considered giving her fake eyebrows, glasses, wigs and black lipstick to the costume consignment store.
2. Every good party has flying monkeys, singing fish and goat cheese.
3. Sheena admires Oprah, Elvis and the Easter bunny.

ANSWER KEY, PAGE 49, THE DINKY DOLLAR
Punctuate

Will Trade:
Have moody, adventurous, well-trained, talented aardvark to trade for gas grill or large stand-up hairdryer. Can't wait to meet you! Drop by at 345 South Dimwood Avenue, evenings.

Garage Sale Tomorrow:
Selling brownies, watch, cordless phone, wire snips, car radio, sneaker laces, computer printer cable, printer, hot dog maker, bicycle tire pump, handle for lawn mower, blade sharpener and ant farm.

For Rent in the City:
Small, cozy, cheap, no frills, fragrant, windowless apartment above Spanky's Garage on 103rd Street. $590/mo. Call 555-3334.

Write Your Own
Answers will vary. Here are a few possibilities.

Moving to Florida. Must get rid of snowboard, mink coat, Green Bay Packers crock pot and wool knickers.

New girlfriend sale. Must sell G.I. Joe collection, cow slippers, Metallica CDs and Cindy Crawford posters.

Starting diet. Selling for cheap: deep fat fryer, potato chip stash, candy thermometer and set of butter knives.

ANSWER KEY, PAGE 50, REVIEW
Punctuate

1. He used to be good at golf, good at tennis, and good at being a nagging menace.
2. She used the phone to call her mother, to call her boyfriend and to scratch a little itchy spot in the middle of her back.
3. Desmond hates sauerkraut, pancakes, onions, mussels and mint-flavored salami.
4. Nobody knows if you are lying, pretending, exaggerating, prevaricating or just kidding.
5. Jungles are hot, noisy, sweaty, wet, dangerous places with no decent theme parks.
6. On my last trip to Australia, I boxed with a kangaroo, trained a dingo to fetch, swam with a platypus and came home with a chunk of the Great Barrier Reef lodged in my foot.
7. Nobody trains a chimp, buys it new clothes, teaches it to read recipes and then sends it off to cooking school without a hand-carved spatula!
8. If anybody cared about my feelings, worried about my worries or shared my joys, pains, hopes and fears, then maybe I wouldn't want to move all the way to New Guinea in the fall.

Write Your Own
Answers will vary. Here is one possibility.

As I stared at the tater tot casserole, the mushy green beans, the wilted cole slaw and the prunes dusted with powdered sugar, a lump of nausea formed in my throat.

ANSWER KEYS

ANSWER KEY, PAGE 51, QUIZ
Punctuate

1. Ben's favorite breakfast is cold pizza, grape juice, Froot Loops and a banana.
2. At the yard sale, Melody found a fencing sword, an hourglass, a huge pine cone Christmas tree and three plastic bullfighters.
3. Joel used soup cans, plastic spoons, a bicycle chain, aluminum foil and orange suspenders to make a self-propelled toaster.
4. Rice cakes can be used as a source of carbohydrates, as coasters for paper cups, as life rafts for hamsters and as earrings to go with "big hair."
5. If I had a million dollars, I would buy a pizza factory, rent an island for a month, hire a butler to wait on me and send my big sister away to boarding school.
6. Mark went to Chicago to learn basket weaving, cat grooming, ear piercing and worm management.
7. Dorothy hates flying mammals, loves clicking her heels, dislikes high winds, mistrusts talking trees and enjoys a good bowl of chicken salad with parsley.
8. If I lived on an island, I would send messages in bottles, eat turtle burgers, sleep in a palm tree and drink coconut milk three times a day.
9. I can't believe you told Marcy about my dog, my cat, my mother, my fish and my false teeth!
10. Don't miss the exciting, exhilarating, mystifying and amazingly brilliant new film called *The Broccoli Murders*.

Write Your Own
Answers will vary. Here is one possibility.

I wanted that llama so badly that I sold my comic book collection, my life-sized cardboard Han Solo and my SuperSoaker water gun to buy it.

ANSWER KEY, PAGE 52, FORS AND NORS AND SUCH
Punctuate

1. Last year I was a space alien in a Christmas play, but this year I'm an ornament.
2. Marvin hated vitamins, for his mother always made him take them with a liver milkshake.
3. Kate weaseled out of the bake sale, yet I still think she would make a great leader for our Ducks Anonymous meeting.
4. Mel's mother raises geckos but refuses to cook them.
5. Elizabeth absolutely loves peanut butter and pickle sandwiches, but she won't touch any other kind of sandwich in the world.

Write Your Own
Answers will vary. Here are a few possibilities.

1. Last night I was awakened by a weird splashing sound, but I couldn't tell what it was.
2. I tiptoed around the house, and I tried to discover where the noise was coming from.
3. Finally, I stumbled into the bathroom, and I saw my cat doing the breast stroke.

ANSWER KEY, PAGE 53, COMMAS AND COMPOUNDS
Punctuate

1. Al pushed a cucumber off the roof, but it bounced off a baby carriage and landed on a dachshund.
2. I do not believe in Munchkins, nor do I think they can dance in real life.
3. Nobody saw the car coming, and no one tried to warn the poor pigeon trying to cross the street.
4. People laughed and shouted at her as they drove by, but Jennifer cheerfully kept rinsing the giraffe.
5. She is not against fast food, nor is she in favor of the slow stuff.

Write Your Own
Answers will vary. Here is one possibility.

Brenda and I were at Wendy's last night enjoying a late-night Frosty. All of a sudden the door opened, and the cutest guy we had ever seen walked in to the restaurant. He went to the counter and ordered a spicy chicken combo meal, and he, of course, had it biggie-sized. Lucky for us, the hunky stranger came and sat with us. We knew he was not from our school because we did not know any guys that were *that* good looking. When we asked him where he was from, he would always change the subject. After he left the restaurant, Brenda joked, "That guy must be from another planet, for he was so cute and so polite." Sure enough, we looked out the window just in time to see the stranger board a mini flying saucer and take off.

ANSWER KEY, PAGE 54, REVIEW
Punctuate

1. I'm about to say goodbye to the city where I was born and raised, and I won't miss it a bit.
2. Nobody can make a chocolate shake or an oatmeal-raisin cookie like Kent, but I would sure like to try after I take that cooking class I signed up for.
3. I'm all for sports and entertainment and goofing off, but you haven't got a chance with that stupid chicken-racing scheme!
4. You may cheerfully eat the cauliflower and tuna sandwich I served you, or you can sit quietly and eat nothing at all.
5. By the way, students may not wear boots in the gym, nor may they ride bikes in the bathroom.

Write Your Own
Answers will vary. Here are a few possibilities.

1. I love my cat very much, but I hate cleaning up her hairballs.
2. My cat, just like my older brother, sleeps all day, yet she parties all night.
3. My cat loves tuna straight out of a can, but she refuses to eat tuna salad sandwiches.

ANSWER KEY, PAGE 55, QUIZ
Punctuate

1. You can mail the application to the address at the top of the instruction sheet, or you can use your computer to fill out an on-line application.
2. Dr. Shawna McCoy graduated from Harvard with a degree in medicine, but one day she decided to give up her medical practice and become a jockey!

3. My sister and I spent seven hours shopping at the mall on Saturday, yet we couldn't find anything that seemed quite right for Dad's birthday present.
4. Jessica couldn't see why her mother had to be so unreasonable about her weekend curfew, nor could she see why her father had to be so unreasonable and agree with her mother about it.
5. Ed loved sailing more than just about anything else in the universe, yet he lived half a continent away from an ocean.

Write Your Own
Answers will vary. Here are a few possibilities.

1. Salamanders are really cute, but they are just too slimy.
2. Shortstop is the best position in baseball, and the Yankees' Derek Jeter is the best-looking shortstop in the world.
3. *Sesame Street* is for kids, but I know a lot of teenagers who still watch it.

ANSWER KEY, PAGE 56, DATES, ADDRESSES AND TITLES
Punctuate

1. The twins were born on July 13, 1987, in the hospital at 45601 Mulberry Street, Hereford, Colorado 80732.
2. Brian Stile, Jr., cut a new album on November 14, 1998, in Nashville, Tennessee.
3. On August 4, 1991, Barry Almaretto, Ph.D., had the first brilliant, original idea of his life.
4. On the morning of September 12, 1994, the house at 123456 Whelton Drive, Hillville, Idaho, was picked up by a twister and set down again somewhere in Montana.
5. I lived at 340 West Pile Street, Newark, Alabama, before I started sleeping at the cheese factory.
6. Dear Madeline,

    Will you marry me? If not, will you at least go out to dinner with me?

    Love,

    Ted

ANSWER KEYS

Write Your Own

Answers will vary. Here is one possibility.

If you want some really good chili to celebrate your birthday on January 11, 2011, let your nose lead you to 57 South Center Street, Chugwater, Wyoming 82210.

ANSWER KEY, PAGE 57, QUIZ
Punctuate

1. Candace Cornflower, D.V.M., spends a lot of time at her animal clinic designing diets for overweight condors.
2. On October 4, 1942, Malcolm's grandparents built a house on the ranch at 2214 Highway 184, Kelby, New Jersey 08888.
3. Dear Will,
   I am all alone in the apartment since you and Jasper moved out. I think I like it a lot better.
   Sincerely,
   Hector
4. If you could travel ahead to September 14, 4078, would you bring your MP3 player or a thermos full of Gatorade?
5. Melvin Schwinnbaum, Jr., is in charge of the talent show this year.

Write Your Own

Answers will vary. Here is one possibility.

Attention all hot wing connoisseurs: You are invited to a Hot Wing Tasting Party. The party will be held on May 5, 2000, at 257 Tabasco Lane, Dixon, New Mexico 87527. Don't forget to bring your handi-wipes, bibs and fire-eating courage. No wimps, please.

ANSWER KEY, PAGE 58, COORDINATE ADJECTIVES
Punctuate

1. The little black kitten sat on a mitten.
2. Black and blue marks lined the top of his cranium.
3. Old, nasty bread crumbs are better than no crumbs.
4. Even with her tall, beautiful sister beside her, Anna was outstanding in a crowd.
5. I once lived in an ancient, leaky hut in the middle of Borneo.

6. Keep your dark and dangerous eyes to yourself.
7. He was in an aging, crippled car when it sailed off into the lake.
8. Black and white stop signs lined the roads of the strange city.
9. Only eager, energetic candidates have a chance at becoming President.
10. Without a cold hard look at the facts, I can't make a decent decision.

Write Your Own

Answers will vary. Here is one possibility.

I never want to go camping again after watching the realistic, nightmarish *The Blair Witch Project*.

ANSWER KEY, PAGE 59, QUIZ
Punctuate

1. The long hard road to success is traveled by many soles.
2. The dark, terrifying mansion was the only building we could see for miles.
3. If you like chicken nuggets, you'll like these sweet spicy balls of broccoli.
4. What really matters is that you become an intelligent, hardworking postman.
5. You can't go to the movies in that lopsided, ridiculous hat.

Write Your Own

Answers will vary. Here are a few possibilities.

1. I hated babysitting for the Klingmans' weird, obnoxious children.
2. They would always play stupid, ridiculous pranks on me.
3. The Klingmans, however, paid the highest, best rates in town.

ANSWER KEY, PAGE 62, REVIEW 1
Punctuate

1. By the time Abe got there, which was well after midnight, the ape was gone.
2. Frankly, Frank, I don't care if you're the slowest rat in the race.
3. Finding flies, catching flies and eating flies is a frog's favorite after-school activity.
4. The circus, I'll have you know, is a perfect place to go for a tightrope experience.

5. On August 4, 1991, Sam Benham had the first brilliant, inspirational idea of his life.

6. Rodney, watch out for that tea cup!

7. A person should never loan money to a relative, in my opinion.

8. Of all the roller rinks in the world, Angela, Bernice, Andrea, Sabrina, Melissa and Ramona had to walk into mine.

9. Delores likes peanuts more than anything.

10. Antonio, because of his size, almost emptied the pool when he did a belly flop.

11. By coming together like this and learning to put up with each other, we learn to be better Boy Scouts.

12. I'm going to a wild west camp this summer, but I am not allowed to bring a camera to record the misery.

13. You will be able to produce your own bagel-making video when you get enough time, when you get enough money and when you get enough courage.

14. Los Angeles, the "City of Angels," contains movie stars, artists, dancers, singers, playwrights and the footprints of that little, mischievous alien E.T.

15. To tell the truth, I don't really care for Uncle Tim's barbecued tuna burgers.

16. For a refund on Wasted Watermelon concert tickets, write to Horace Townsend at 33522 River Muck Way, Heartache, Alabama 36543.

17. Dear Dad,

    Please send me some money. Pretty please.

    Your loving son,
    David

18. I had a long, weary, agonizing wait in the dreary office of Wilma Hipple, M.D.

19. Mrs. Bender gave her son two tickets to see a Norwegian comic opera, the one called *The Valiant Snow People.*

20. I'm not a psychiatrist or a doctor, but let me give you some advice, Mario.

Write Your Own
Answers will vary. Here is one possibility.

The door bell rang last Saturday, and I opened the door to the most interesting character. Amazingly, a used portable dishwasher sat on my front porch, and a skinny little man in a turban sat on top of it. He said he was the Sultan of Scrub sent to end all of my dishwashing miseries. Of course, that immediately grabbed my attention. I looked down at my dishpan hands and invited the sultan in. Once I realized that the portable dishwasher was not worth more than a paper plate, I tried to nicely get rid of the skinny salesman. He, unfortunately, could not take a hint. After he had been at my house for a couple of hours, I had to turn to more blatant methods. We ended the evening with me screaming at the top of my lungs, hurling a portable dishwasher and swinging a sultan through my screen door. Everything wasn't all bad, however. I did get a load of dishes washed.

ANSWER KEY, PAGE 63, REVIEW 2
Punctuate

1. Yes, Lynette hates beef, cheese, carrots and anything green, at least when she eats at home.

2. Chauncy, don't you know what a chifforobe is?

3. The Pillsbury Dough Boy, the Munchkins, the Seven Dwarfs and my friend Teresa are all famous for being shorter than a coffee table.

4. Incidentally, I want you to bring me the flyswatter.

5. Dear Madeline,

    In your last letter you insulted my dog, threatened my cat and lied about the dent in my car. Don't write again.
    Angrily,
    Meredith

6. Incidentally, when are you going to have a good, long, serious look at the junk on your back porch, Aunt Eunice?

7. Because insects have grown immune to many bug sprays that are on the market all over the world today, people have been relying on flytraps.

8. Here are some flowers, my little pumpkin, for your birthday.

9. Before my mother could get to him, he was bound up like a mummy.

10. Before you came into my life with your wonderful gooseberry dumplings, I could never gain any weight, Pierre.

11. Nobody believed Clarissa when she announced that March 3, 1094, was an important day in history, but she went on to prove that she was right with two books and a magazine article.
12. You can call me Fred or Jed or Ned or Ted or nothing at all, Melissa.
13. Your brother, incidentally, got married last night in Reno.
14. Alvin, always an innocent bystander, was run over by a wandering woman with a shopping cart.
15. Nobody but Wally Thomas, Jr., my unusual next-door neighbor, can eat a pizza under-water.
16. All of Santa's letters were mistakenly sent to 1689 Rutemeyer Street, Anchorage, Alaska 99543.
17. I won't eat peas, however.
18. I can't believe you or your mother or your father didn't recognize Grandma's parrot, the green and red one named Bilbo.

ANSWER KEY, PAGE 64, TEST
Punctuate

1. He was broken down, weary and tired of pre-school.
2. Nobody keeps lettuce crispier and greener than Edith Tupperware, my grandmother.
3. The boss wants Daniel to wash the windows on the thirty-third floor.
4. If you want a ride to the mall this evening, you had better help me with these dishes.
5. Everybody in town over 60 years old is at the town's biggest celebration, the Librarians' Overdue Dance.
6. Nobody in school, nobody at home and nobody in the chess club knew that I had joined the bell choir.
7. Oliver, I thought I might mail you some dental floss.
8. If you do every single page of your math homework every night and pass all the remaining tests with at least 99%, you might still manage to pass the class.
9. Kristina and Carleta, to tell you the truth, aren't the ones I would pick to win.

10. For your own good, if you'll just exercise, eat right, sleep tight and wash your fruit, you will live a long and healthy life.
11. If all goes well, you should be in Madagascar by morning, Brett.
12. You are a healthy, vibrant, young bunny, yet I see a weakness in your hopping technique, Ernest.
13. A pink cloud hung in the sky above the crowd watching the championship soccer match, and it stayed there throughout the game.
14. Emily Rodder, M.D., and Frank Wall, Ph.D., decided to quit their jobs and set up a Go-Kart track at 6793 Kingston Drive, Waterhole, Mississippi 38681.
15. I kept falling asleep while we read that rag-gedy, boring book about Sir Chuck, who was some kind of knight.
16. Cara, don't torment your little brother.
17. Ashley was exhausted by the time she left the pound, incidentally.
18. His sister, the one who lived at 3409 Bruiser Lane, Handown, Ohio, threw him a "new idea" party and invited all his old, rich, annoying friends, including Charles Oldhow, M.D.
19. Dear Ms. Zesbaugh,
    Please excuse my absence. I stayed home because I felt so good today.
    Your student,
    Alissa
20. Sarah didn't want to wear the mustard-colored cardigan her sister had knitted for her, and she also didn't feel much like put-ting on the pink skirt her mother had made to go with it.

Printed in the United States
by Baker & Taylor Publisher Services